**THE
46 RULES
OF
GENIUS**

THE 46 RULES OF GENIUS

AN INNOVATOR'S GUIDE TO CREATIVITY

TEXT AND ILLUSTRATIONS BY MARTY NEUMEIER

NEW RIDERS
FIND US ON THE WEB AT WWW.NEWRIDERS.COM
TO REPORT ERRORS, PLEASE SEND A NOTE TO ERRATA@PEACHPIT.COM
NEW RIDERS IS AN IMPRINT OF PEACHPIT, A DIVISION OF PEARSON EDUCATION

ACQUISITIONS EDITOR	**PRODUCTION EDITOR**	**DESIGNERS**
NIKKI ECHLER MCDONALD	DAVID VAN NESS	BROOKE KLASS
		CYA NELSON
PROOFREADER	**DESIGN DIRECTOR**	IRENE HOFFMAN
LIZ WELCH	MARTY NEUMEIER	BERYL WANG

ISBN 13: 978-0-133-90006-4
ISBN 10: 0-133-90006-1

9 8 7 6 5 4 3 2 1

PRINTED AND BOUND IN THE UNITED STATES OF AMERICA

THE

46

RULE

OF

GENIUS

An innovator's guide to creativity

MARTY NEUMEIER

In honor of
Saul Steinberg
and
E. B. White

To most people, a genius is someone with a towering IQ—say 140 points or higher. This is simplistic. A genius is more than that, but also less. In practice it only takes an IQ of 125 to become a genius. What you need beyond that is a facile imagination and the skills to apply it, driven by a passionate will toward a focused goal.

A genius doesn't start out as a genius at *everything* but a genius at *something*. For example, you can be a genius at molecular biology, or a genius at reading people's feelings. You can be a genius at programming software, or a genius at broken-field running. This puts genius-hood within the reach of nearly everybody. Over time, a genius may connect several *somethings* into a semblance of *everything*, but this is optional in the definition of genius.

In my recent book *Metaskills*, I laid out five talents we'll need to thrive in an age of increasing man-machine collaboration. These talents, which I've called metaskills, are *feeling*, or empathy and intuition; *seeing*, or systems thinking; *dreaming*, or applied imagination; *making*, or design talent; and *learning*, the ability to acquire new skills. None of these needs a high IQ. What they need is a high regard for creativity. The rules in this book are creative rules. They're general guidelines to help you envision, invent, contribute, and grow.

Then what's a genius? Here's my working definition: A genius is any person who turns insight into innovation, and in the process changes our view of the world. In other words, it's *someone who takes creativity to the point of originality*. The philosopher Arthur Schopenhauer said it best: "Talent hits a target no one else can hit; genius hits a target no one else can see."

The rules in this book are as timeless as they can be. None of them are new, yet they can help you *create* something new. Michelangelo didn't invent the hammer and chisel, but by using these tools he sculpted the *Pietà*. Just as you can't shape a block of marble with your bare hands, you can't shape ideas with your bare mind. You need rules. Rules are the tools of genius. Use them when they help; put them aside when they don't.

I've purposely written a concise book. Most of the creative people I know are consumed by their projects, and reading a long book is a luxury they can't always afford. So here's a slim volume with bite-size advice. You can reach into it randomly, underline its salient points, return to the rules as needed.

I make no claims of completeness for *The 46 Rules of Genius*. Instead, I've chosen to focus on the principles most often ignored, forgotten, or heedlessly broken. It starts with some advice on strategy—or how to get the right idea. It continues with practical tips on execution—how to get the *idea right*. From there it moves to building your creative skills over time, and finally to putting your brilliance to work in the larger world.

Caution: *The 46 Rules of Genius* is not for everyone, for the simple reason that not everyone can be a genius. This is not usually a failing of native intelligence. It's more likely a lack of a) will, or b) skill. I presume you have a good supply of a), or you wouldn't have this book in your hand. As to b), you'll need a little help—and a healthy appetite for work. Happily, work is not really work when you're investing in what you love.

My fondest wish is that you'll combine the desire you already have with these time-tested principles to ignite an endless cycle of creative growth: your desire will drive your learning, and your learning will fuel your desire. This is the magic that makes a genius. If you accept this as a central premise, the rest will follow.

—*Marty Neumeier*

CONTENTS

Part 1   How can I innovate?

Part 2   How should I work?

Part 3 How can I learn?

Part 4 How can I matter?

*There is
no great genius
without a mixture
of madness.*

–Aristotle

PART 1 **HOW CAN I INNOVATE?**

You've probably heard that it's unwise to break the rules until you know how to use them. You've probably also heard the opposite—there *are* no rules—it's the job of innovators to disregard convention. Which of these is true?

Oddly, both. This is the Genius Paradox. You have to disobey the rules of creativity to obey the rules of creativity. And in obeying the rules of creativity, you automatically disobey the rules of creativity. That's because the number one rule is to break the rules.

Creative rules are not rigid dictates but rough principles—patterns that a variety of artists, scientists, and thinkers have used for centuries as the scaffolding for their inventions. You shouldn't be a slave to them. You don't need to keep them in your conscious mind. But having considered them will broaden your repertoire for any creative challenge that calls for a full response.

Here's how to resolve the Genius Paradox:

1) React to the rules by embracing them or breaking them.
2) Observe the results.
3) Rewrite the rules from your own experience.

You'll find that there *are* rules for creativity—*your* rules. They may not be the ones that others follow, but they'll be true and useful to you.

One caveat: Make sure your new principles are not just scars from a previous experience—it's easy to draw the wrong conclusion from a single failure. Weigh your newly forged rules against the rules of the ages to make sure they have the heft and hardiness to do the job.

Rule 2 **WISH FOR WHAT YOU WANT**

Wishing is like a warm-up sketch for problem solving. When you let your mind wander across the blank page of possibilities, all constraints and preconceptions disappear, leaving only the trace of a barely glimpsed dream, the merest hint of a sketch of an idea. To start wishing, ask yourself the kind of questions that begin:

> How might I...?
> What's stopping us from...?
> In what ways could I...?
> What would happen if...?

From there you can ask follow-up questions like:

> Why would we...?
> What has changed to allow us to...?
> Who would need to...?
> When should I...?

At this stage there's no reason to place limits on your wandering. What's the *can't do* that you wish were a *can do*? The future problem you could start solving now? The half-baked notion you'd like to see a reality? Where's the place where the suddenly possible meets the desperately necessary? Wishing allows you to leave the realm of limitations, if only for a few moments, to imagine a future worth pursuing.

Rule 3 **FEEL BEFORE YOU THINK**

Don't jump into planning as soon as you've sighted a goal. Learn to be still and listen. Pay attention to the nagging voice. The uneasy stomach. The barely felt longing. Your subject may have something to tell you.

Resist the temptation to impose a cookie-cutter solution on an intriguing problem, or a groundbreaking solution on an insignificant problem.

Hold back until you've had enough time to sort through your feelings and consider the issues. Depending on the nature and scope of the challenge, this could take five seconds or five days. It takes what it takes.

Have you ever noticed that when you're searching for facts, you'll cast your eyes downward as if the information were on the table? And when you're trying to invent an answer, you'll look upward as if the solution were on the ceiling? These are commonly observed tendencies in problem solvers. But when you're trying to access your intuition, *looking* won't help at all. You'll need to *feel*.

Feeling your way to a solution is like an athlete deciding his or her next move. It happens more in the body than the brain. It gives you direct access to your intuition so you can bypass the usual fears, distractions, default solutions, and ego traps that can make your work less than brilliant. Feeling lets you forge a connection with your subject that mere thinking can't reach.

Close your eyes and drift with the problem. Let it talk to you. Imagine you're a psychologist, and the problem is your patient. Listen carefully. Give it your deepest empathy and fullest attention. Be available to the problem. Don't try to fix it. Feel your way forward.

One of the skills that separates a leader from a follower is the ability to see what *might* be, but so far *isn't*. Most people can see what's already there. You don't need magic glasses to see that the Eiffel Tower is a popular tourist destination, or that the area of a rectangle is the product of its height and width, or that millions of people will pay extra for a fancy cup of coffee. But you do need magic glasses to see what's still missing from the world, since by definition what's missing is invisible.

The trick is to notice what artists and designers call *negative space*. It's the plain background of a painting, the white space on a printed page, the silence between lines of a play, or the rests within a musical score. In the world of art, these are purposeful elements of composition. In the marketplace, these are crevices that harbor opportunity.

Try these three techniques for discovering the negative space in a marketplace, a problem, or a situation.

Sift through threats for hidden possibilities. Every threat carries with it the potential for innovation. The problem of obesity contains the possibility of new kinds of nutrition. The problem of global pollution contains the possibility of new energy sources. The problem of high unemployment contains the possibility of new educational models. The list is endless, if you can learn to see what's not there.

Examine sectors for uneven rates of change. The future is already here, goes the saying—it's just distributed unevenly. Look for areas that have changed, then look for similar or adjacent areas that haven't changed. Search for pockets of resistance to successful new ideas. Chances are, it's only a matter of time before change comes. Why not be the catalyst?

Imagine how a growing trend might affect an established norm. Make a list of nascent and dominant trends, then mentally apply them to industries, businesses, and activities that haven't changed for a long while. What will the trend toward organic farming mean for fast-food restaurants? What will mobile payments do to retail shopping habits? How might nanotechnology change the energy market? How will always-on computing change the college experience?

To find out what's not there, look for the job *not* done, the road *not* taken, the product *not* made. These are the magic glasses that let you see the invisible and conceive the inconceivable.

Figure out what type of problem you're solving.
Is it a simple problem? A complex problem?
A structural problem? A communication problem?
A technology problem? A political problem? A leadership problem? A design problem? A budget problem? Unless you know what type of problem you're solving, your solution will be wrong, no matter how well you seem to solve it.

For most of us, the problems we tackle are given to us by someone else—a boss, a teacher, a client, a committee, an organization. While the problem may seem logical in the way it's stated, a little bit of probing may reveal a faulty framework.

The framework is the boundary drawn around it, the "rope of scope" that keeps it from sprawling to infinity. It narrows the focus, suggests a direction for the work, limits the investment, and determines how success is measured. If the framework is wrong, everything else will be wrong.

Your first impulse may be to accept the problem as stated. Resist. Be curious. Ask questions. Probe further. While it may seem disrespectful or annoying to pester your problem-giver with too many questions at once, that doesn't mean you can't raise them mentally and marshal your thoughts for a later conversation. In fact, you may not even *have* any questions at first. Sometimes questions need time to surface.

As you become more proficient at accepting assignments, you'll find questions like these helpful:

Have we seen this problem before?
What do we know about it?
Are the boundaries the right boundaries?
Are we even solving the right problem?
Should we solve a bigger problem instead?
If we succeed, what will be improved?
What will be diminished?
What will be replaced?
What opportunities will it spawn?
Who stands to gain and who stands to lose?
Do we need to solve the problem at all?
Who says? So what? Why not?

By asking these types of questions, you may find that the boundaries of the problem were drawn too small—the actual problem was more important, and the only reason to minimize it was to shrink it to fit a budget, a time frame, a job description, or a skill set. While these may be issues, it's better to face them head on and make them part of the brief.

Or you may find that the frame was drawn the right size, but around the wrong challenge. The first question in creating something new is not *how to*, but *what to*.

Rule 6 **FRAME PROBLEMS TIGHTLY**

There's a widespread myth that genius needs a large canvas. Yet every creative person knows this to be untrue. Too much freedom can lead to mediocrity. Why? Because without boundaries there's no incentive to break through them. A real genius has no difficulty redefining a brief or defying convention. It's second nature. But give a creative person too much freedom, and you'll get a final product that's over-designed, over-worked, over-budget, and under-focused. The greatest gift you can give a genius is limitation, not license.

The basic principle is this: A tightly structured brief will generate energy; a wide-open one will drain it. When creative people get into trouble, it's not because they can't see the *solution*—it's because they can't see the *problem*.

Here's a formula for framing a challenge in a way that lets you clearly see it:

1. *Write a problem statement.* Summarize the challenge in a brief paragraph, then describe the

most likely outcome if it's not addressed.

2. *List the constraints.* Constraints are creative limitations imposed by the problem. Is there a funding limit? A time limit? A technological barrier? A political barrier? A business constraint? A brand constraint? A knowledge gap? Competitive hurdles? Limitations are important because they tighten the frame and point to solutions.

3. *List the affordances.* Affordances are creative possibilities that exist within the problem. While constraints close the door, affordances open a window. Constraints and affordances shape the space where new ideas can dance. What's missing from the market? What are the capabilities I can call on? Who do I have on my team? How can the technology be advanced? What does the problem tell me? Inside every problem is a hidden solution.

4. *Describe success.* Your problem statement suggests the most likely outcome of doing nothing. Now describe the most likely outcome if your solution succeeds.

Learn what geniuses have discovered throughout the centuries: A problem well-framed is a problem half-solved.

The human mind loves either/or choices. We prefer a choice of A or B. Yes or no. Chicken or beef. Simple choices give us a feeling of control, while open-ended choices give us a feeling of unease. Therefore we'd rather choose *between* than *among*.

By the same token, we prefer to break complex problems into separate parts. It's easier to focus on a single part than to hold a complex problem in our brain. Yet without a good view of the whole problem, it's hard to see how the parts fit together.

To complicate matters further, we're easily fooled by our emotions and intuition—the very instruments we rely on to guide us through the thickets of problem solving.

The fact is, the human mind is a mass of biases. Beginners are fooled by what they believe; experts are fooled by what they know. And the biggest bias of all is believing you're not biased.

The counterweight to bias is thinking in whole thoughts instead of fragments. Squint your mind to blur the details. Look for how the parts of the problem fit together. View a complex situation from a variety of angles so you can see the hidden connections and surprising possibilities.

Start by examining it from three basic positions:

First position, or the view from your own vantage point. Easy, but not always trustworthy.

Second position, or views from the vantage points of other relevant players. More difficult, requiring empathy and observation.

Metaposition, or the view from outside the system. The most difficult of all, requiring objectivity and critical thinking, which don't come naturally to most of us.

The term for this "unnatural" style of thinking is *systems thinking.* It's a method of understanding complex problems by studying the relationships of the parts to the whole. It's a way to see the big picture and how it changes over time, more like watching a movie than viewing a snapshot.

Systems thinking lets you solve problems by respecting their context. For example, when designing a chair, consider the room it will be in. When planning a room, think about the house it's part of. When conceiving a house, respect the community it belongs to. When managing a community, consider the environment it's supported by.

When you think in whole thoughts instead of fragments, you create solutions, products, or experiences that resonate with the larger world, and thereby create broad, sustained value.

The "dragon pit" is the gap between *what is* and *what could be*. It's a space filled with discomfort, darkness, and doubt. Most people would rather grab the first rope thrown to them—*what is*—rather than stay and fight the dragons guarding *what could be*. But *what could be* is where the ideas are. A genius is someone who can tolerate the discomfort of uncertainty while generating as many ideas as possible.

The unresolved conflict we find in the dragon pit is actually a prime source of creative energy. The gap between vision and reality produces creative tension, which can only be released by a new idea. Without creative tension, there's no need to push forward to an alternate reality. Inevitably, the result of tension-free thinking is business as usual.

The secret of creativity is to keep your ideas in a "liquid state." Let them mutate, morph, and recombine as they bump into one another. Avoid the tyranny of *no* and the naïvete of *yes*, all the while holding onto the hopefulness of *maybe*. Often this requires courage, especially when the stakes are high. The cave you fear to enter, goes the ancient proverb, holds the treasure you seek.

Creative thinking requires that you leave the

known and venture into the *unknown*. This can be difficult if you're deeply knowledgeable about your challenge, your discipline, or your industry. The known is an attractor state, a default position that pulls your mind like a magnet.

When you find yourself stuck in your own knowledge, get unstuck quickly. Ask yourself why you're stuck. Is it a lack of information? If so, get it. A lack of skills? Go develop them. Is it that the solution doesn't exist? Move on to the next dragon.

Rule 9 **APPROACH ANSWERS OBLIQUELY**

The hallmark of innovation is surprise. No surprise, nothing new. Nothing new, no interest. No interest, no value. Therefore, creating surprise is a crucial step in creating value through innovation.

The first step in surprising others is to surprise yourself. This can be maddingly difficult, since you already know most of what you're likely to think of. You may need to trick your mind into new modes of thought by using one or more of the following techniques. Nine approaches can help you make connections between seemingly unrelated ideas:

Think in metaphors. A metaphor is a relationship between two dissimilar things: "The world is a stage." By comparing the world to a stage, you can more easily imagine that we're all actors playing a part—an insight you might not have had without the metaphor.

Think in pictures. Visual thinking can strip a problem down to its essence, leading to profoundly simple connections that language by itself can't make. The ability to draw stick figures, arrows, and talk balloons is all you need to think visually.

Start from a different place. When you grab for the "correct" solution, brilliant solutions will elude you. You'll get stuck in the tar pits of knowledge, unable to free your mind of what you already know. The easiest way to escape this trap is by rejecting the correct solution—at least temporarily—in favor of the "wrong" solution. While the worst idea can never be the best idea, it will take your imagination to a different starting place.

Steal from other domains. If you steal an idea cleverly enough, the theft will go unnoticed. While stealing is not as hard as exercising pure imagination, it still takes a mental leap to see how an idea from one industry or discipline could be adapted to another.

Arrange blind dates. Great ideas are often two ideas that haven't previously been introduced. Using a technique called "combinatory play," you can throw unrelated ideas together to see if they create a new idea. Look for combinations that have a natural fit.

Reverse the polarity. Write down as many assumptions about the problem as you can think of. Reverse them. Think about what it would take to make the reversed assumption true. Some of these may lead to new ideas.

Ask simple questions. What else is this like? Who else believes this? What if I changed it slightly? What can I eliminate? What can I substitute? Is this the cause or the effect? What if I changed the timing? What if I made it bigger? What would happen if I did nothing?

Watch for accidents. You can sometimes make the best discoveries when you're searching for something else. Pay attention to anomalies, surprises, or feedback that confounds your expectations. These can open up exciting new areas of inquiry.

Write things down. Not all your ideas will be worthwhile, but they may trigger new ideas. Make a list of your thoughts as you work through any problem. Keep a notebook, a sketchbook, a scrapbook, or an idea file. A pencil can be a crowbar for lifting ideas from your subconscious.

When the right idea comes along, your emotional brain sends a signal to the rest of your body. It's a tingle, a flash, or a jolt that tells you something remarkable has happened. Suddenly the world reels, a thousand gears snap into place, and the long-hidden answer appears, shimmering, before your disbelieving eyes. Developing a sensitivity to these signals is an integral part of being creative.

But what if your idea is only new to you, and not to the rest of the world?

And how do you know if it's any good in the first place? Here's where it helps to apply the six tests of originality:

1. *Is it disorienting?* A great idea should be unsettling—not just to you, but to others in your group. Some people may reject it on the spot. This may be a good sign, since the potential of a new idea is often inversely proportional to its comfort factor.

2. *Does it kill ten birds?* A good idea kills two birds with one stone. A great idea kills ten or twenty.

3. *Does it need to be proved?* If an idea doesn't need to be tested, it's probably because it's not very original or not very bold. The skepticism that calls for a proof of concept is one of the signals of originality.

4. *Is it likely to force change?* Great ideas are not polite. They never say they're sorry. They don't try to fit in. On the contrary, they force the rest of the world to change in self-defense.

5. *Does it create affordances?* The measure of a great idea is the quantity and quality of *affordances* it throws off. Affordances are the opportunities inherent in an idea. The more affordances—for customers, a company, an industry, or society at large—the better the idea.

6. *Can it be summarized?* A great idea can usually be described in a sentence. It has a strong internal order, one that answers to a clear and compelling purpose. If you find it hard to describe your idea, stop working on your description. Fix your idea.

Rule 11 **USE BEAUTY AS A YARDSTICK**

The world's greatest scientists, philosophers, and artists agree: If an idea isn't beautiful, it probably isn't innovative. They're putting a special spin on the concept of *beauty* by defining it as a quality of wholeness, or harmony, that generates pleasure, meaning, and satisfaction. A beautiful idea is often a great idea.

While beauty can't be reduced to a pat formula, it can be understood by seeing it as a system

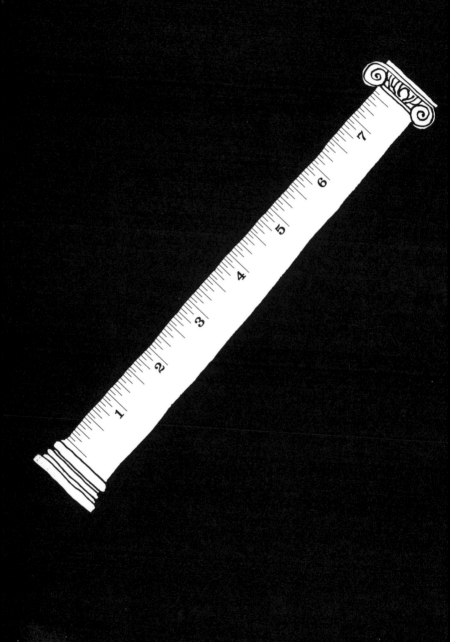

containing three interactive elements: *surprise,* *rightness,* and *elegance.*

In everything we experience as beautiful, there's a moment of *surprise* when we first encounter it. Surprise is the jarring pop of disrupted expectations— the "jolt" of rule #10. The pleasure, meaning, or satisfaction that follows this jolt can be experienced as a warm glow, a slowly spreading smile, or the hair standing up on your arms. Physiologically, it's a blast of serotonin to your central nervous system.

Rightness, the second element of beauty, is a kind of fitness for duty, a specific structure that lets the thing we're encountering align with its purpose.

Elegance, the third element, is a rejection of superfluous elements in favor of simplicity and efficiency. An elegant idea is one that has the fewest number of elements that allow the whole to achieve its purpose. The best ideas seem so perfect that they leave no room in the imagination for anything better.

When all three of these elements are working well together, an idea has enormous potential to improve the context in which it exists.

How can you bring beauty into your work? By shaping it according to the principles of design. Anyone can be a designer. All you need is the will—and the skill—to change an existing situation into a better one. The next section of the book lays out the rules.

A BEAUTIFUL IDEA IS OFTEN A GREAT IDEA.

You boil it in sawdust:
You salt it in glue:
You condense it with locusts and tape:
Still keeping one principal object in view—
To preserve its symmetrical shape.

—Lewis Carroll

PART 2 **HOW SHOULD I WORK?**

The first 11 rules were concerned with getting the right idea. The next 14 are concerned with getting the *idea right*. This is the work of bending, shaping, and polishing your idea so it aligns with its purpose. This is the point at which you go from thinker to maker.

The default setting for traditional thinkers is to reach a decision as quickly as possible. In business, for example, managers tend to rely on a two-step process: *know* and *do*. They know something—from a case study, a book, an article, a best practice, a previous experience—and move straight to doing something. The flaw in this process is that it cuts out the possibility of new ideas. The know-do process is incapable of finding new approaches or mitigating risk, so it plays safe. It says: Just do what worked in the past, and nothing more.

A better way to reach a decision is to *make* one. When you insert *making* between *knowing* and *doing*, you put new ideas on the table. You invent models, prototypes, or mockups that can be tested before they're selected. Making lets you *design* the way forward, instead of merely *deciding* the way forward. Deciding is much easier with a range of tested possibilities to choose from.

The know-make-do process is at the heart of design thinking, the discipline at the core of innovation. It's the process of changing an existing situation to a new and better one. Design can be applied to an organization, a product, a building, or a policy. It can improve a career, a habit, a skill, or a relationship. Anything that can be changed can be designed.

Yet new ideas are fragile. They can't stand up to withering criticism or the careless opinions of so-called devil's advocates. Rejecting a new idea because it's not immediately successful is like giving up a baby because it can't hold a job. New ideas need to be protected and nurtured. They need time to be shaped, tested, corrected, and polished.

Does this mean that the know-make-do process will slow down decision making? Maybe yes, maybe no. But it beats the know-do process, which is guaranteed to produce suboptimal results. When you're trying to innovate, it's best to design quickly and decide slowly. Hold your fire until you see a worthy target.

The starting point for choosing a process is understanding what kind of situation you're dealing with. Is it simple or complex? Are the elements static and unchanging, or dynamic and unpredictable?

Many projects have fairly static elements. Even a project as complex as making a movie can be approached as a collection of simple parts. You can break the movie down into scenes, then break the scenes into shots and camera moves. Once you have a script in hand, it's easy to see how the scenes will fit together, at which point you can shoot them in whatever sequence you like. You can feel confident that the scenes will make sense when they're assembled into a finished product.

Another example is the manufacturing process. Manufacturing gets its efficiencies from predictable steps. Some steps can be completed simultaneously, whereas others must be completed sequentially. But all the steps involve static parts that can be assembled at the end. You can then repeat the process endlessly, make small improvements over time, and scale it up when you're ready.

These are examples of a linear process. There are many situations in which it works perfectly, such as producing an instruction manual, mounting

A

↓

B

↓

C

a legal defense, or planning a wedding. In each of these cases, you might expect surprises and setbacks, but only a few that would require rethinking the entire project.

On the other hand, you can't approach a musical composition in the same linear way. Any sequence of notes you add will change the character of the whole composition. Every new element suggests changes to the other elements, keeping the whole piece in constant motion. When you try to pin it down, it fights back. It's alive and dynamic.

The same can be said of building a business, managing a brand, or designing an app. These are complex activities. They require a dynamic process.

Rule 14 **USE A DYNAMIC PROCESS FOR REACTIVE ELEMENTS**

Complex problems are reactive. They don't hold still while you work on them. The conventional approach is to address a complex problem as if it's a simple problem, breaking it into discrete steps that can be executed one at a time. Too often the result is 1) a solution that doesn't address the real problem, 2) a solution that causes new problems, or 3) a solution that's largely ineffective. Just because you've ticked the boxes doesn't mean you've solved the problem.

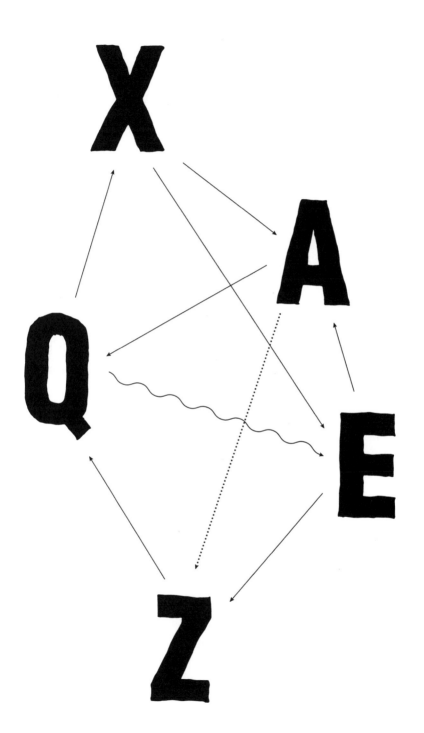

Complex projects with interactive elements—parts that change dynamically with every change to the whole—require an all-at-once process instead of a step-by-step process. The way this unfolds depends on what the project is.

Let's take the case of building a brand for a new product. A brand is a customer's perception about a product, service, or company. Therefore the task of brand-building is to give customers experiences that help them perceive your product in a favorable way. The proof of success is not the number of boxes you've ticked, but the change in the way customers think about the category in which you're competing. You want customers to rank your brand as number one or two in your category, not as number five or six.

The experiences you design for customers might include the product itself, a series of messages about the product, and a certain way the product is packaged, sold, or delivered. You might build in features that delight customers enough that they tell their friends or write positive reviews online. You might also train front-line employees to represent the brand in a way that makes customers happy. You might design a program to encourage loyalty, rather than risk losing customers to competitors. Beyond all this, you might want to imbue these elements with freshness and imagination, so your brand becomes a hard act to follow.

Creating a program with this level of complexity has more in common with writing music than baking a cake. If you try to address these elements one at a time, you're likely to end up with a "Frankenbrand," a collage of experiences that customers perceive as mismatched and inorganic.

A better process for designing a complex program is to address all the elements at once. Let the various parts influence each other dynamically as they emerge from your mind or your pencil or your team's whiteboard markers. Let them crash into each other and create new elements. Keep them in a liquid state long enough to see them morph and mutate into surprising new possibilities. Stir them until they blend into a seamless whole, one that's more than the sum of its parts.

When employed by teams, this free-for-all process is known as "swarming." It's fast-paced, exhilarating, and well-suited to small teams of creative professionals. It's also disconcertingly chaotic. Swarming is not for the faint of heart.

Every design has its own order. The job of the genius is to discover it. The best approach is to start with a logical structure, then deviate from it according to your needs, your skills, and the particular demands of your project.

If you're designing your own house, for example, the combination of site, neighborhood, budget, space requirements, and your personal taste may suggest a three-level, modernist cliff-hugger to take advantage of the views and adapt to its special engineering needs. Or it may lead you to design a farmhouse-like compound that blends into its setting and accommodates a range of specific uses. Every set of circumstances dictates a different underlying order.

If you're developing a website, parameters may include your skill set, your audience, their experience level, the navigational possibilities, and your brand's personality. The functional purpose of the website may point to a magazine-style format with rich, emotion-laden photography. Or it may suggest an all-typography format with no-nonsense navigation and clear copywriting. Avoid cookie-cutter approaches. Every design should align with its unique purpose.

This doesn't mean that every project should be produced lavishly, or that it should break the mold on general principle, but simply that each project has a hidden structure that, if discovered, can bring out its full potential. When purpose and structure find the right fit, one and one make three.

Rule 16 **EXPRESS RELATED ELEMENTS IN A SIMILAR MANNER**

The principle of *grouping* brings clarity to any design by signaling the purpose of each element. Related elements should look alike, and unrelated elements should look different.

For example, the designer of a smartphone app can create a similar look for each of its functional icons, expressing that these functions are of the same type or have the same level of navigational importance.

The leader of a company can direct the actions of employees by organizing her expectations into a long-term purpose, a medium-term mission, and a series of short-term goals, so every employee knows what to do, when to do it, and why.

The writer of an instruction manual can indicate various levels of information by grouping the instructions according to steps, diagrams, captions, cautions, and tips. Steps can be numbered, diagrams drawn in blue, captions shown as italics, cautions displayed in boxes, and tips marked with stars.

The goal of grouping is to simplify understanding so that the user—or the reader, the listener, the viewer, the follower, the citizen—can interact with a design intuitively instead of having to interpret the intentions of the designer. In other words, the designer should do the hard work to make the user's work easy.

By the same token, you should express unrelated elements in a different manner. If the dashboard in your car featured a large panel of look-alike buttons—five for the wipers, twelve for the radio, two for the headlights, seven for the air conditioner, and so on—you would find these difficult to learn without consulting the manual every time. But when each of these functions is placed into different groupings, they quickly become intuitive.

There's a reason supermarkets organize their items by affinity. With over 20,000 products, shoppers would find the store hard to navigate if all the boxed products were shelved together just because they were in boxes. We tend to categorize grocery products by their use, not by their container types. The ketchup is next to the capers because both are condiments. The walnuts are next to the flour because both are baking ingredients.

Organizing, designing, and leading all benefit from a high degree of clarity. The way you group things can determine how well they're understood.

Rule 17 **MATCH FORM TO FUNCTION, FUNCTION TO FORM**

Form doesn't always follow function. Sometimes it works the other way around. The rule is simply this: form and function should be inseparable. When the shape of something matches its intended purpose, the marriage seems inevitable, as if no other combination could exist. This is the *rightness* component of beauty, the quality that sends clear signals of authenticity, integrity, honesty, and wholeness.

Reflect on the inevitability of a hammer, with its sculpted metal head and curved claw, and a handle shaped to fit your palm. Or the strong, angled strokes of an uppercase A, immediately recognizable as the first letter of the Roman alphabet. Or consider the intuitive gestures of a touchscreen interface that lets you scroll, swipe, click, or rotate. Think about the design of a business in which customers, employees, owners, and suppliers all get something they want, and are happy to give something valuable in return. These are examples of form and function in perfect alignment.

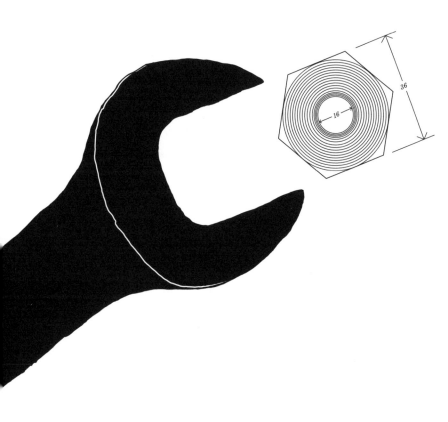

Put yourself at the mercy of your material. Feel its desire. Spin the wheel of your imagination until the ball stops on the right answer. When you find the match, you'll feel a tiny thrill of satisfaction. Tune your sensitivity to this feeling, and learn to be dissatisfied until you find it.

This is not to say that a real genius would never purposely mismatch form and function. But even so, the mismatched pair would be a good match if it fulfilled its purpose. Remember, rule number one is to break the rules.

Rule 18 **DON'T BE BORING**

The most common killer of a bright idea is a dull execution. Boredom interferes with understanding. It lets the mind wander as it searches for something to care about. It fails to engage the emotions of the audience, turning their experience into a tedious intellectual exercise.

The antidote to boredom, unsurprisingly, is surprise. The element of surprise is the most powerful weapon in the creative arsenal. It confounds our expectations and rivets our attention. It makes competing stimuli fade into the background as we focus on what suddenly seems important.

Surprise can take the form of drama, shock,

wit, or even extreme beauty. It can take the form of contrast: dark vs. light, big vs. small, fast vs. slow, simple vs. complicated, and so on. It begins with a perceptual event—we notice something different—which then triggers an emotion. If the emotion is strong enough, we may store it as a memory and assign a meaning to it.

Some examples of creative surprise:

The punch line at the end a joke
A burst of sweetness in a savory dish
An invention that disrupts an industry
A fancy word in a plain sentence
A quiet movie interrupted by a gunshot
A flashback in a fast-paced novel
A tender ballad sung in a rough voice
A sudden outburst of obscenities
A huge sculpture of a small subject
Self-deprecating humor
A frozen moment in a dance routine
A staid product with a new feature
A brutally truthful observation

Of course, if you overuse the element of surprise, it's no longer surprising. It becomes the very background noise you had hoped to overcome. Surprise is your secret weapon. Use it strategically.

CREATIVE SURPRISE IS YOUR SECRET WEAPON.

The rule for surprise is this: Direct the most attention to the most important part of your idea. Don't sprinkle surprise around randomly, or the result will be scattered attention and a loss of focus.

Some examples of using surprise to direct attention:

You write a particularly catchy musical sequence for a pop song. You make sure the most important lyrics are contained in that sequence.

You add an exciting new feature to a product. You make sure the feature underscores your brand's most compelling difference.

You design a trademark for a business. You make sure the strategic uniqueness of the business is reflected in its symbolism and form.

Your movie script has an emotionally charged scene. You make sure the scene creates a turning point or encapsulates the main theme.

You make a slide presentation. You save your most compelling point for your most dramatic slide.

You write a headline for an ad. You place the most powerful word at the end of the sentence.

While these examples may seem obvious, their lessons can be easily forgotten in the heat of creation. It's not too late to make changes after

the first draft or the first pass. In fact, that's usually the best time to do it—after you see what you've got, and before you present it to others.

Rule 20 APPLY AESTHETICS DELIBERATELY

Aesthetics is a collection of tools, such as shape, rhythm, contrast, scale, color, and texture, used to create and appreciate beauty. Most creative people have a natural affinity for aesthetics, learning through experience the various tricks and techniques that produce the effects they're looking for. They often apply these techniques unconsciously, without ever using the word *aesthetics*.

Other people would just as soon throw the whole notion of aesthetics out the window. They contend there are no universal laws for creating beauty, and anyone who says there are is not a true artist.

But aesthetics is not a book of laws. It's more like a box of toys. When you play with these toys, applying them to your project in various ways, you'll find they can bring clarity, excitement, and nuance to your work. Some of the more universal ones are shown on the facing page.

If these aesthetic principles seem abstract to you, it's probably because you haven't felt their weight in your hands or applied them consciously to real tasks.

SCALE

DETERMINE THE SIZE OF AN ELEMENT OR COLLECTION OF ELEMENTS TO BEST ACHIEVE ITS PURPOSE

SEQUENCE

PLACE ELEMENTS IN A CHRONOLOGICAL ORDER TO CONTROL HOW INFORMATION IS REVEALED OR EXPERIENCED

RHYTHM

ARRANGE THE PACING OF A SEQUENCE TO IMPART EXPERIENCES SUCH AS INTENSITY, SPEED, CALMNESS, OR AWKWARDNESS

TEXTURE

EVOKE EMOTION OR CREATE INTEREST BY ADDING TACTILE QUALITIES SUCH AS ROUGHNESS, SMOOTHNESS, BUMPINESS, STICKINESS, OR PATTERNING

CONFLICT

INTRODUCE DISSONANCE, DISCORD, OR ANOMALY TO CREATE EMOTIONAL TENSION OR PROVOKE INTELLECTUAL INTEREST

GESTURE

USE A SPONTANEOUS FLOURISH TO IMPART A FEELING OF MOVEMENT OR DESCRIBE A PHYSICAL ACTIVITY

TENSION

SET UP CONFLICT BETWEEN TWO OR MORE ELEMENTS TO CREATE EMOTIONAL INTEREST

CONTRAST

EMPHASIZE THE DIFFERENCES BETWEEN ELEMENTS TO CREATE DRAMA, CLARIFY A POINT, SHOW PROPORTION, OR INDICATE HIERARCHY

SYMMETRY

USE A MIRROR-IMAGE BALANCE TO MAKE AN OBJECT OR COMPOSITION TO CREATE STABILITY, CALMNESS, OR DIGNITY

PERSPECTIVE

CREATE AN ILLUSION OF PHYSICAL SPACE OR DETERMINE THE CLOSENESS OR DISTANCE OF ELEMENTS

GROUPING

PLACE ELEMENTS TOGETHER OR ARRANGE THEM INTO A PATTERN TO INDICATE A RELATIONSHIP

SHAPE

CREATE THE FORM OR EXTENT OF AN OBJECT BY DRAWING ITS BOUNDARIES

BALANCE

ARRANGE ELEMENTS INTO A PLEASING WHOLE TO CREATE SATISFACTION, EFFICIENCY, OR FAIRNESS

AMBIGUITY

COMBINE INCOMPATIBLE MEANINGS OR EXPERIENCES TO TRIGGER NEW MEANINGS OR EXPERIENCES

HARMONY

ARRANGE THE ELEMENTS OF A COMPOSITION SO THAT THEY ARE COMPLEMENTARY RATHER THAN CONFLICTING

With enough practice they'll begin to make sense and become powerful extensions of your creative skills. Aesthetic choices are never right or wrong, just better or worse. Try them and see.

Rule 21 **VISUALIZE WITH SKETCHES, MODELS, OR PROTOTYPES**

Our intuitive responses to new problems don't always work. When you move directly from *knowing* to *doing* something, you can easily find that your response is inadequate, off-target, or wrong. This is because what worked for one problem doesn't always work for another.

But when you add the middle step of *making*, it changes not only what you *know*, but what you're likely to *do*. It's the imagination-based step of creating a range of hypotheses that you can prototype, test, and refine. The more ideas you can prototype, the more you'll learn about the possibilities of your problem. When ideas flow, the music of chance plays faster.

Get your mind and hands working together. Make a sketch, construct a model, or assemble a prototype. Then another. And another. With each attempt, you'll reveal new possibilities for innovation. Your mind will talk to your hands, and your hands will talk to your mind. This dialogue is called *generative thinking,* and it happens only when you're making something. It's the active ingredient of design.

But what if you have no drawing skills? What if you're all thumbs? What if you couldn't build a sandwich, much less a prototype? You'd be surprised at how little skill it takes to trigger new thoughts. While many challenges benefit from trained hands, other challenges need only the ability to draw stick figures, cut pieces of cardboard, or tape various objects together. The goal is to get the prototypes to talk back, surprise you, and make you think in new ways.

Without prototyping your ideas, you can easily fall back into the *know-do* mode of problem-solving, unable to test whether your ideas will work in the real world. In theory there's no difference between theory and practice. In practice there is.

Rule 22 **EMBRACE MESSINESS**

It's almost impossible to reconcile creativity with cleanliness. The sculptor gets metal dust all over his studio. The writer must wade through a clutter of notes, books, and crumpled drafts to get to her desk. The rock musician must weave through a tangle of cables, black boxes, guitar stands,

and song notes to sit down and create. The business strategist must navigate a thicket of scribbles, arrows, and boxes on his whiteboard while avoiding the distractions of multicolored sticky notes on stacks of must-read articles.

You may find that you can't be creative until you clean up your desk or tidy your workspace. This makes perfect psychological sense. Each new project needs a clean slate. And with each new project you'll need a little extra time to switch mental gears. But once the gears start turning and the project gets moving, the mess is part of the work. Don't worry about it. Don't try to clean it up until you need more space or you're ready to start a new project. Let the mess be a mess.

Organizations that depend on innovation must embrace this reality. They should provide open, flowing spaces that accommodate clutter for extended periods time while their people do battle in the creative dragon pit. Clutter at this stage is not a vice, but a virtue: Messiness is next to godliness. Cleanliness can wait.

Question: How can you predict whether an idea will survive in the real world?

Answer: *Test* it in the real world.

Many entrepreneurs believe you can't test new ideas. The reason they give is that people can't predict what they'll buy or endorse. While this is mostly true, what the entrepreneurs forget is that new ideas are tested all the time—as soon as they reach the marketplace. At this point the shortcomings are apparent and it's too late to fix them.

The solution to this seeming paradox is to expose ideas to the marketplace *before* they're launched. You can do this by approximating real-world encounters using prototypes and a small number of test subjects.

For example, you can gauge the potency of brand messages by A/B testing them with a limited audience. You can assess the features of a new product by handing prototypes to a cross-section of likely users. You can try out a new business model by first opening a store in a small market. You can test the sales potential of a retail package by placing a range of mock-ups on a store shelf,

then talking to customers who are shopping there.

While none of these situations are perfect, they come close enough to real life to provide useful feedback. You don't need precise information to make a confident decision about a new idea. You just need *uncertainty reduction*. Without pretesting your ideas, you have only two options: 1) take a substantial risk and accept the consequences, or 2) reduce the risk by removing the qualities that made it innovative in the first place.

Tip: Don't use focus groups to test new ideas. Focus groups were designed only to "focus" the thinking of product developers and marketers. They weren't designed to predict future sales or judge the market-worthiness of new ideas. Instead of focus groups, use your best creative judgment, build prototypes, and show them to customers, one at a time, in realistic situations.

Rule 24 **SIMPLIFY**

People tend to view simplicity and complexity as opposites. But this isn't strictly true. The enemy of simplicity isn't complexity, but disorder. And the enemy of complexity is also disorder. While complexity seeks order through addition, simplicity seeks it through subtraction.

$$\frac{2}{1}$$
$$3$$

A goal of design is to drive out disorder by maximizing both simplicity and complexity. In most designed products, what we respond to best is a rich, layered experience (complexity) combined with ease of use, ease of understanding, or ease of purchase (simplicity).

Most people have a built-in bias toward addition instead of subtraction. For some reason, the concept of "more" comes naturally to us. Yet the innovator knows that the value of any design doesn't lie in how much is piled on, but how much is discarded. More is more, but less is better.

Here are seven ways to simplify your work:

1. *Test elements by removing them one by one.* A design should have no unnecessary parts or gratuitous elements. See if subtracting an element will hurt the overall design. If it doesn't, remove it.

2. *Discard needless features.* More is not always better. Build your design around one or two main features and keep the others secondary.

3. *Kill vampire elements.* Make sure none of the elements is contradicting a more important one, or drawing attention from the main idea.

4. *Place elements in a logical sequence.* Try numbering the elements to give them a sense of order. Put them into a line, a series, or a time-based sequence.

5. *Group items into buckets.* If the purpose of the design calls for a large number of elements, group them by use, meaning, size, or other organizing principle.

6. *Hide complexity behind a simple interface.* Help people navigate complexity by giving them intuitive controls. For example, the electrical grid is complicated, but a light switch makes it easy to use.

7. *Align elements behind a single purpose.* When all the elements support a simple purpose, the whole design will appear simple.

Works of genius are rarely complicated on the surface. You can describe their greatness in a single sentence, and even embellish them slightly without destroying their simplicity. Such is the power of subtraction. As you learn to simplify, you'll discover that the best design tool is a long eraser with a pencil at one end.

*The illiterate of
the 21st century will
not be those who
cannot read and write,
but those who cannot learn,
unlearn, and relearn.*

—*Alvin Toffler*

PART 3 **HOW CAN I LEARN?**

Learning to learn is a metaskill—a skill applied to itself. It multiplies your knowledge and accelerates your progress. When you learn to be your own teacher, you can acquire any skill you put your mind to. You can quickly build a new skill on the roof of the last one. You can move laterally from one skill to the next by bringing deeply understood principles to related disciplines. The ability to direct your learning is personal growth squared.

Teaching yourself is called *autodidacticism*. It requires that you develop your own theory of learning, a personal framework for acquiring new knowledge. While every person's framework is different, here are ten principles you can use to construct it:

Learn by doing. We learn better and faster when we use our hands, our senses, and our whole bodies in addition to our brains.

Find worthy work. Not all work is educational, important, or fun. Look for work you believe in. It's too hard to work with one hand holding your nose!

Harness habits. The brain forms habits when routines are transferred from the rational level to the automatic level. They allow you to perform familiar tasks with little conscious effort, freeing up mental resources for new challenges.

Focus on your goals. It's easy to become distracted by shiny objects in your periphery. A genius learns to concentrate on a single task for an extended period of time.

Cultivate your memory. While general knowledge is available online, your store of craft-specific knowledge needs to be ready at a moment's notice. Memorize it.

Increase your sensitivity. A key trait of genius is the ability to make subtle distinctions among outcomes. Consciously identify the nuances that separate the truly great from the merely good.

Stretch your boundaries. To keep growing, always aim slightly beyond your current abilities.

Customize your metaskills. Intuition, emotional intelligence, critical thinking, imagination, and other high-level skills can make a big difference in how you learn. Focus on the metaskills that will drive your professional success.

Feed your desire. When you want something so badly that you never give up, success eventually surrenders to you. Keep the fires of passion burning with books, articles, talks, and conferences.

Scare yourself. Take on projects and responsibilities that lie outside your comfort zone. Look for workarounds to mitigate your fears. As any genius will tell you, fears faced are fears erased.

FEARS
FACED
ARE
FEARS
ERASED.

Ideology is toxic to learning. As soon as you begin to believe something, the spirit of inquiry dies. If you believe that climate change is unrelated to human activity, there's no reason to change your behavior. If you believe that new technology is always beneficial, there's no reason to question it. If you believe your company is the best in its industry, there's no reason to improve it. Belief is the surest way to stop imagination, innovation, and progress.

There's an old adage: "Seeing is believing." The assumption is that we find it difficult to accept anything as truth until we see the evidence for it. Yet it's far more likely that, for most of us, believing is seeing. Once we believe something, we're all too ready to see it as truth. Pyschologists call this phenomenon *confirmation bias*—a tendency to block out inconvenient facts that happen to contradict our belief system.

A key characteristic of the genius is a strong *disbelief* system. Instead of starting from belief, the genius starts from a position of curiosity, wonder, skepticism, or iconoclasm. The journey leads from the unknown to the known, and, with luck and perseverance, you'll discover new information along the way.

The rule is simple: If you're looking for real knowledge, keep ideology at bay. Pretend you're an alien with no preconceptions about life on Earth. Lean on belief only when necessary. And even then, think of belief as a placeholder for knowledge—not knowledge itself.

Rule 27 **DO YOUR OWN PROJECTS**

Something happens when you work on challenges of your own choosing. Your mind becomes magnetized. It starts to attract little bits of information that can help you solve your problem or complete your project. While a magnetized mind can occur with any kind of challenge, the effect is strongest when the challenge rises from your own passion or your own sense of purpose.

When you do your own projects, you give full play to four capabilities: 1) An abiding passion for discovery and innovation, 2) an ability to shape a large body of knowledge into a coherent system, 3) the skill to translate this system of knowledge into action, and 4) a capacity for deep concentration over an extended period of time.

These are the traits of a genius. Everyone experiences some success in these areas during his or her life. What the genius does is to turn these traits

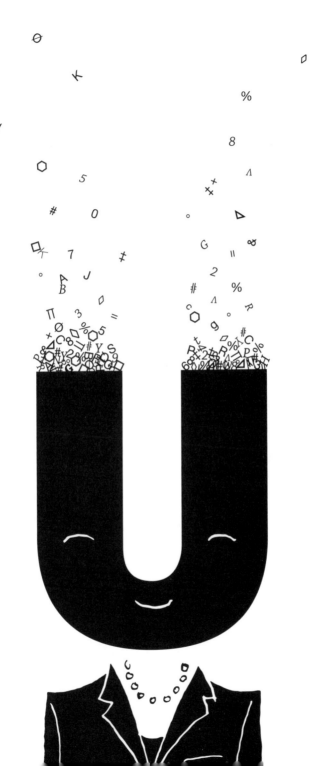

into lifelong habits, which are then expressed as talent. Talent isn't something we have—it's something we do. We develop our skills in the course of working on the kinds of projects, problems, and challenges that address our deepest interests.

While you can't always bend your workplace to your will, you can look for small opportunities on the outside, or after hours, to practice your craft. These experiences, far more than the daily grind of given assignments, will help you reach your creative potential.

Rule 28 **KEEP A HERO FILE**

Students in creative disciplines sometimes worry that they might lose their personal style if they allow themselves to be influenced by teachers, practitioners, or other students. They reason that imitation is the enemy of innovation. They believe that if the unique talent they need isn't there already, it never will be.

There's a kernel of truth to this. But only a kernel. Because the way we actually learn is by standing on the shoulders of others. We acquire skills by watching more advanced practitioners do their work, eventually growing strong enough to support the weight of newer practitioners.

To develop a strong personal style, open yourself to the widest possible range of influences. Look closely at the work of practitioners, groups, and cultures you admire. Appreciate with felonious intent. When you see something you wish you had done, copy it, photograph it, tear it out, take notes on it; put it in a file, pin it to a board, tape it into a book, or keep it on a shelf. Your natural likes and dislikes will act as a filter, so that the examples you collect will begin to resemble your future style.

Every time you start a new project, revisit your hero file and use the examples as benchmarks for quality. Don't quit working until you've achieved something as good as one of the items you admire.

Of course, standing on the shoulders of giants is one thing. Clinging to their pant legs is another. Make sure you steal the principles that underlie their work and not the work itself. Outright copying teaches very little. Learning to extract and apply principles is the path to genius.

Rule 29 **INVEST IN YOUR ORIGINALITY**

The ability to produce original work is a rare and valuable asset. It lies at the heart of innovation, strategic differentiation, and societal progress. It imparts a quality of "never-before-ness" that can command attention, fill voids, and create wealth. By definition, you can't be original by copying an original. You have to start from a different place.

Originality doesn't come from factual knowledge, nor does it come from the suppression of factual knowledge. Instead, it comes from the exposure of factual knowledge to the animating force of imagination. Imagination is the ability to conjure mental images, sensations, or concepts without perceiving them through the senses. Everyone is born with this ability, but the genius is a person who cultivates it, applies it, and invests in it. Imagination is a learnable skill.

Depending on the quality of your knowledge and the level of your imagination, originality can fall into four quadrants: 1) ideas adapted from the same domain, 2) ideas adapted from a different domain, 3) ideas that are new to yourself, and 4) ideas that are new to the world.

If you have a little knowledge and a little imagination, you might be able to borrow an idea from a competitor and adapt it for your own purposes. While not truly original, it can nevertheless contain enough freshness to get the job done. You can take comfort in Voltaire's claim that "originality

IMAGINATION

NEW TO YOURSELF

NEW TO THE WORLD

ADAPTED FROM THE SAME DOMAIN

ADAPTED FROM ANOTHER DOMAIN

KNOWLEDGE

is nothing more than judicious plagiarism."

But let's say you have a bit of experience, and your subject knowledge is fairly broad. By applying a small amount of imagination to your larger knowledge base, you might be able to adapt an idea from a different domain—another industry, discipline, or culture. In this case your originality would be of a higher order, less like plagiarism and more like appropriation.

Or maybe you have much less knowledge, but a well-developed imagination. You might be able to invent an idea you've never encountered before. Although others may have invented the same idea without your knowing it, the ability to imagine "new to you" ideas is the first step toward being an original thinker.

As you accrue more knowledge and you exercise your imagination with deliberate practice, "new to you" can become "new to the world." At this point you've seen enough to know what has and hasn't been done, and inventive enough to fill the gap with a surprising idea.

Originality is more than judicious plagiarism. It's the ability to dream, to disassociate your thoughts from the linear and logical and end up someplace new. And like many skills that were once thought to be inborn, it must be learned.

You can learn anything, but you can't learn everything. Be careful what you take into your brain-attic, since there's only so much room up there. Pick your subjects with a sense of purpose.

For example, if your goal is to bring a cinematic quality to video games, you should stuff your brain with the history of film, graphic novels, and representational art. You should pay attention to dance, sports, and music. You should master the digital tools of your trade, and take a strong interest in emerging technology. While you can certainly take up dog training on the side, starting a whole second career in dental hygiene would probably slow your progress.

It's a competitive world, and the best way to outrun your competitors is to outlearn them. This doesn't mean burning the midnight oil week after week, month after month, head buried in books or eyes glued to various screens. It's not about the quantity of your knowledge. It's about strategic alignment. Does your learning line up with your goals? Will it lead to fresh insights or deeper understanding? There's plenty of time to learn everything you need to know, as long as you learn strategically and not randomly.

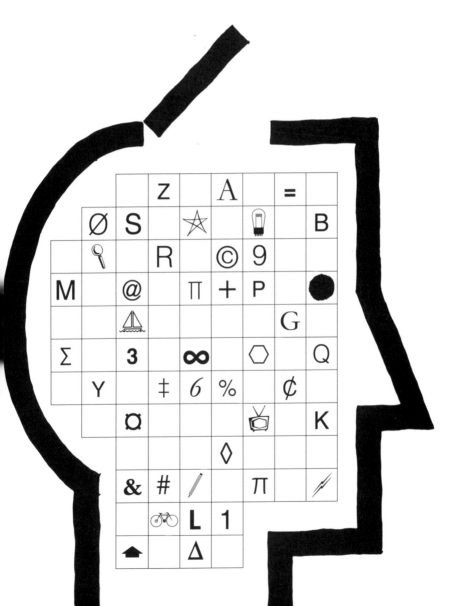

Over the long haul, *how* you learn is more important than *what* you learn. When you know how to learn, you start to use the most powerful metaskill of all. It's the self-awareness that comes from observing what you think while you're thinking it. "Metacognition" tells you when and how to use a particular strategy to get the most useful knowledge, right when you need it. It saves time and energy, which you can then apply to more learning, which in turn saves more time and energy. Great for you, great for your dog.

Rule 31 **SHORE UP YOUR WEAKNESSES**

There are two contradictory schools of thought on developing skills. The first is to build on your strengths and forget about your weaknesses. The second is to strengthen your weaknesses until your report card is all *A*s. Unfortunately, both schools of thought fail to nurture your inner genius.

The truth is, brilliant people often start with a lopsided skill set. They fall in love with a subject or activity for which they have a special knack, then keep adding to their skills while letting other subjects or activities slide. This creates a canceling effect: they get good at what they love, but their lack of ability in other areas limits their success.

Think of the engineer without the right people skills, or the entrepreneur who can't balance a checkbook.

The remedy for lopsided brilliance is to simply shore up your deficiencies and not try to eliminate them. You don't need the skills of an orator to be a thought leader—just original ideas and the courage to deliver them from a podium. You don't need the drawing skills of a Leonardo da Vinci to be a great painter—just a grasp of aesthetics and a vision for the next big thing in art. The idea is to neutralize your weaknesses so your strengths can operate unfettered.

The concerns of a genius fall into three main areas: 1) originality (applied imagination), 2) craft (mastery of tools), and 3) efficiency (getting things done). If you're like many creative people, you're strong in only two of these areas. All you need to do is neutralize your weakness in the third. For example, if you're strong in originality and craft, prioritize speed. If you're strong in craft and efficiency, prioritize originality. If you're strong in efficiency and originality, prioritize craft. By shoring up your weakest area, your genius is free to soar.

When your work contains an element of joy, you
learn faster. This is called *ludic* learning, or learning
by playing. What makes it so effective is the space
it allows for positive emotions. Emotions drive attention, and attention drives learning. Physiologically,
creative play releases endorphins, tiny molecules
that put you in a good mood. When you're happy,
you're more creative. When you're unhappy, you lose
access to your intuition. Happiness and creativity
are mutually supportive.

How do you know when you're in the joy zone?
When you lose track of time and all you can think
about is the work itself. This doesn't mean that your
task suddenly seems easy, or that you're aware of
having fun, but that you're completely absorbed
in your challenge. You're working in the Goldilocks
channel: not too easy, not too hard—just right.
People in this state can learn new skills up to ten
times as fast as those who are anxious (with a
too-difficult task) and those who are bored (with
a too-easy task). Long hours become short hours
when your work is playful.

It's generally acknowledged that creativity seems
to happen "out of time," as if the clock doesn't
matter. What's less acknowledged is that creativity

actually requires this condition to flourish. Creativity simply takes as long as it takes. The more you try to rush it, the less you achieve. The less you try to rush it, the more you achieve. You can't reasonably expect to have an epiphany by 11:45 or an innovation a week from Tuesday. But if you forget about the clock, you may well have an innovation a week from Tuesday, if not sooner.

Creative learning assumes freedom—the freedom to find the right balance between your personal ability and your challenges. You have to identify your strengths, discover the right medium in which to express them, and allow yourself the necessary time to experiment and push the limits of your understanding. Ludic learning is often the doorway to genius.

Rule 33 MAKE EDUCATIONAL MISTAKES

In the realm of creativity, mistakes aren't mistakes. They're clues. Each one reveals a part of the mystery you're trying to solve.

The fact is, if you already knew how to proceed with a project, you wouldn't need creativity. You could just follow the recipe, read the manual, or tick the boxes. Creativity is the discipline you use when you don't know the answers, when you're

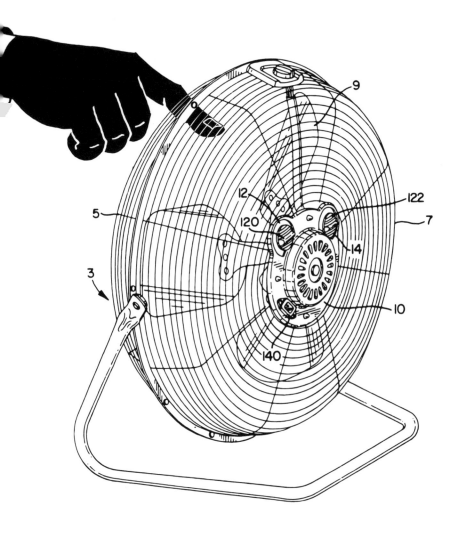

traveling to parts unknown. On this type of journey, missteps are actually steps. Every mistake brings you closer to the solution.

But here's the catch: You have to make bold mistakes. Smart mistakes. New mistakes. Because if you only do what you've always done, you'll only get what you've already got. You have to try, fail, and learn. Then try something new, fail a different way, learn more.

When you make a prototype, you're making a prediction—a testable assumption that lets you see what works and what doesn't. This is not unlike the way your brain works. It continually makes predictions against reality while your dopamine cells keep score. Before your predictions can be right, they have to be wrong. A wrong prediction then becomes a "wake-up call" that your dopamine cells convert into an emotion, which is stored in your memory as knowledge. The stronger the emotion, the stronger the memory.

One of the benefits of purposeful failure is a gain in resourcefulness. Often the most resourceful person is the one who has tried the most approaches, taken the most risks, failed the most times. The continuous process of trying, failing, and learning builds up a wide range of responses that can address a variety of problems.

MAKING ANYTHING STARTS BY MAKING MISTEAKS.

The lesson for innovators is this: Instead of fearing failure, embrace it. Fail big. Fail often. Keep trying. Remember that making anything begins by making mistakes.

Rule 34 **SEEK INSTRUCTIVE CRITICISM**

When you're working in creative mode, you're more likely to be imaginative and intuitive. But you're also more likely to make logic errors. Switching back and forth between creative mode and critical mode is difficult, since it requires considerable mental and emotional effort. The best cure for logic blindness is to seek regular feedback from people who can critique your ideas *instructively* rather than *constructively*. It's your job to be constructive—you're the maker. What you need from them is a clear view from the outside. Ideal critics are those who will:

1. Listen to your idea, ask questions, and not react too quickly.

2. Strive to judge your idea against your specific intent.

3. Summarize your idea in a way that seems fair and even insightful.

4. Identify any aspects of your idea that they agree with or appreciate.

5. Finally, identify aspects that they question or find lacking.

In the real world, however, the feedback you get may be reactive, subjective, negative, or less than insightful. Sometimes you'll find it possible to erase the doubts of naysayers with a slight modification to the work. Resist the temptation to argue. Try to understand your critic's position, do your best to act on any advice, and always express your gratitude. Even off-target feedback can be instructive if you approach it objectively. What doesn't kill your project can make it stronger.

Rule 35 **FUEL YOUR PASSION**

Creativity doesn't respond to *time* management so much as *passion* management. Passion—the deep excitement you feel about your subject, your project, your profession—is the engine of creative genius. While you only get a certain amount of time in each day, you can expand your passion nearly without limit. You can pump it up, stretch it out, increase its intensity—all with a bit of management.

The key to passion is to treat it as a resource, like a savings account or a kitchen garden. If you want to maintain a bank account, you need to make deposits. If you want to keep a vegetable garden, you need to tend your plants. If you want to feed your passion, you need to invest in your projects, your learning, and your inspiration. The investment can come in the form of reading, seminars, workshops, internships, pro bono work, time off, or simply doing projects you love. The goal is to return to work refreshed and renewed.

But where does passion come from? Do some people have more than others? Is the game somehow rigged? The best answer is that each of us is born with a certain capacity for it, and then we develop it according to our abilities and desires.

You may be the kind of person who falls deeply in love with a subject overnight but has trouble maintaining interest for more than a few months. Or maybe you're the opposite: a person who takes a long time to develop an interest but then stays with it for decades. There are some people with so many interests they can't seem to focus on one, and others who grapple with periodic depression, unable to stay excited about anything at all.

While everyone's situation is different, the principle is the same: Passion drives creativity. Fuel it, protect it, tend it, grow it. Manage it as the renewable resource it is.

Rule 36 DEVELOP AN AUTHENTIC STYLE

Everyone has a personal style of working, but not everyone has a "good style." Good style grows out of good taste—an appreciation of the way aesthetic principles determine beauty. Think of your taste as an ability to recognize what's beautiful, and your style as the way you apply your taste. Personal style is unique by definition—it responds to a variety of factors, including your goals, your profession, your training, your culture, your life experiences, and the quirks of your personality.

But what about good taste? Is it personal or universal? Here we wade into muddy waters. When it comes to taste, it's impossible to separate the personal from the universal. Still, it may be helpful to think of good taste as a universal ideal, an understanding of aesthetics that crosses all boundaries by addressing our deeply human need for delight. Those who are trained in the principles of aesthetics are more likely to notice the presence of good taste wherever and however it occurs. A Ming vase is beautiful whether you're Chinese, German, Australian, or Icelandic. A J-class yacht would be as beautiful to a thirteenth-century peasant as a twenty-first-century sailor.

Those who are untrained may "feel" the presence of good taste, but not necessarily recognize it as such. They're more likely to define good taste as only what's fashionable, lavish, elaborate, or expensive.

Good taste is often none of these things. It's the knowledge of how aesthetics can make a designed object or outcome more of what it should be, and less of what it shouldn't.

Furthermore, you can't buy good taste. You can only earn it through effort. Good taste, unlike beauty, is not in the eye of the beholder. It's universal.

Good style, however, is particular to the person creating the work. *Your* personal style is different from *my* personal style.

In developing an approach to work, resist the temptation to *put on* a style by adopting "stylistic" elements—such as overusing jump cuts in a movie, or always wearing one red sock. Reject all mannerism, ornament, and affectation. The route to style runs straight through authenticity, simplicity, and directness.

Now, here's a secret: A good personal style will mostly come from your limitations, not your strengths. It's the result of working around your shortcomings, using all the aesthetic skills you can muster. Since your limitations are unique to you,

BE YOURSELF. EVERYONE ELSE IS TAKEN.

your style will also be unique. This is what people find most fascinating about stylish people. They're uniquely and delightfully themselves. We can look to Oscar Wilde for the best advice: "Be yourself. Everyone else is taken."

Rule 37 **PRACTICE**

All creativity contains an element of craft, a set of *making* skills that connects aesthetic judgment with creative tools. The musician needs to turn her instrument into an extension of her mind and body. The furniture designer needs to get a "feel" for his equipment and materials. The CEO needs to master a wide range of reports, metrics, and control mechanisms. The software engineer needs to make his development tools second nature. The writer needs to develop an "ear" for vocabulary, grammar, and punctuation.

Without the skills of your craft, you might be able to come up with original ideas. But you'd have difficulty making your ideas stick—demonstrating, developing, testing, and sharing them. Skills bridge the gap between thinking and making. There are no skills without practice—practice is the exercise gym of genius.

But what kind of exercises do you need? It's obvious that a concert pianist will need to practice scales for many hours a week. It's not so obvious what an app designer should practice. The fact is, there are as many ways to practice as there are practitioners. It's up to you to decide what skills you'll need to build, and then what kind of exercises you'll use to build them.

Whereas *what* to practice is specific to your craft and your goals, *how* to practice is universal. Here are seven tips for mastering the art of practice:

1. *Control your environment.* Have a regular place to work—a room, a shop, a desk, a lab, a studio, or a quiet corner with a comfortable chair. Find a space where you can work without interruption.

2. *Practice consciously.* High-level skills don't come from mindless repetition. They come from intelligent repetition—doing something over and over while thinking about how to improve. If you're conscious of your actions now, they'll become mindless good habits later.

3. *Set aside a regular time.* If you try to fit practice sessions into random time slots, your progress will be slower than if you practice on a schedule. You might not need much time—15 minutes, 45 minutes, maybe an hour—depending on the skill you're trying to learn.

I will not practice mindlessly.
I will not practice mindlessly.
I will not practice mindlessly.
I will not practice mindlessly.
I will not practice mindlessly.
I will not practice mindlessly.
I will not practice mindlessly.
I will not practice mindlessly.
I will not practice mindlessly.
I will not practice mindlessly.
I will not practice mindlessly.
I will not practice mindlessly.
I will not practice mindlessly.
I will not practice mindlessly.
I will not practice mindlessly.
I will not practice mindlessly.

4. *Take baby steps.* It's better to learn in easy stages than in one big practice session. Practice, take a break, practice, take a break, practice, take a break. You'll find that after each break, your skills will be stronger.

5. *Make your exercises fun.* Design your sessions to be games. Keep them light, change them around, invent new rules, play around with them. As soon as you make practice a chore, the learning goes right out of it.

6. *Seek feedback.* Learning any skill depends on a feedback loop. You try something, then you measure the result against a goal or a standard. With every try, your subconscious is learning what works.

7. *Celebrate small gains.* When you take notice of your gains, you learn more joyfully and more eagerly. Take a moment to appreciate them when they happen. You'll find that small improvements add up quickly.

The age-old riddle,
What is the meaning of life?,
turns out to be astonishingly simple:
The meaning of life is meaning.

— Mihaly Csikszentmihalyi

PART 4 **HOW CAN I MATTER?**

Passion is a powerful thing. But it's not always strategic. We live in a society where competition creates winners and losers. Unless you apply your passion to a unique purpose, you're likely to be squeezed out by equally passionate competitors. It's a cruel world. But it doesn't have to be if you master "nichemanship"—the art of dominating a specialty that's unavailable or uninteresting to others.

None of us is born with a purpose, but nature has equipped us with goal-seeking minds that let us perform better in the context of one—a sense that life *means* something. It's the belief that we matter, that we're making a positive contribution to society. The best way to make a contribution is to find the overlap between what you have to give and what the world needs.

You may be passionate about acting, for exam-ple, but the theater doesn't need another actor. It has plenty of actors, and thousands more waiting in the wings. What the world needs is a remarkable actor. It needs an actor who is exceptionally good, exceptionally different, or special in some useful way. If you want to be an actor, you need to find out what the profession needs, then decide whether

you alone can be the solution. If you can't, you may end up as one of thousands who compete away each other's chances for work.

The fastest way to find your niche is to pay attention to what makes you different. This is counterintuitive for students and beginners who assume that what's different about them is what needs to be corrected. As you enter the workplace, it pays to find out which of your flaws might actually be features. The actor who loses key roles to charismatic competitors might prove highly successful in supporting roles. The family practice physician with a so-so bedside manner could end up as an exceptional medical researcher. The corporate manager who has trouble staying focused might be surprisingly effective as an entrepreneur.

The best strategy is to choose a direction that lets you work with your whole heart instead of a divided heart. Overcommit to a mission that fits your interests, stretches your abilities, and gives you the potential to make a difference. If a thing isn't worth doing, it isn't worth doing well. Wholeheartedness confers a distinct advantage upon those who can offer it. It turns ordinary work into extraordinary work, and it opens the tiniest niche to a world of possibilities.

Creativity requires sustained focus. Whether you're working alone or in a group, you need the ability to pay attention. Paying attention is an apt phrase, because it costs something to focus. You pay the price in psychic energy. Most of us can focus on a difficult task for a few seconds or a few minutes, but it's real work to stay in the game much longer than that. Our minds tend to wander, looking for an escape. We can almost feel our brain squirming in its seat.

Difficulty focusing isn't new, but our attention spans are getting shorter as the pace of life speeds up. This is the trap of today's "always on" culture. If we're always on—dealing with distractions, interruptions, and just plain busy-ness—then our creative brains are always off. We're left with partial thoughts, partial experiences, and partial understanding.

This doesn't mean that you should avoid any activity that doesn't align with your mission. In fact, outside interests—and downtime—are just as critical to achieving your goals as direct interests. They serve to round out your skill set and reignite your passion. The point is that creativity takes concentration, the ability to stick with a problem

long enough to get beyond shallow, multiple-choice answers.

Leonardo da Vinci was the very model of focus. By all accounts he was a highly social creature—dressing in the latest fashions, hobnobbing with royalty, attending and designing the most glittery social events—but he would also disappear for weeks at a time, incommunicado, to pursue a line of questioning without interruption. With this discipline he produced a huge body of artwork and invention, plus an extensive series of notebooks that included as many as 100,000 drawings and 13,000 pages of handwritten text.

You can't switch off the world. But you can lock it out temporarily while you work. You can carve out quiet time to think things through by yourself, so that when you return to the world you have something deep and whole to show for it.

Working alone doesn't mean being lonely. It doesn't even mean being alone. But it does mean paying attention, listening to your own voice, and listening to the voices of others with sustained focus. Only when you've mastered this habit can you hope to approach genius-hood.

Creativity takes perseverance: A great idea is not a great idea if no one gets to experience it. What makes creativity especially difficult is that there are so many unknowns. So many judgment calls. So many doubts about the outcome. A genius is the person who can power through the doubts to cross the finish line. Only the strongest are able to bounce back from the false starts, the setbacks, the wrong turns, and the strident voices of naysayers.

This puts the creative genius in the same class as the mountain climber, the triathlete, or the seeker of high office. Without perseverance, all you have is a plan, an intention. You can't win if you don't complete the race.

There are several tricks for overcoming adversity on the long road to creative success:

1) Focus only on the next step.
2) Give yourself a reward at every milestone.
3) When you encounter a setback, label it a setback.
4) Revel in your mistakes and record them for posterity.
5) Remember that all unfinished work seems un-redeemable.

6) Work so fast you won't have time to evaluate it until it's done.

The vast majority of people give up before completing an ambitious personal project. By simply following through—by persevering—you may well find yourself among an elite group of innovators.

Rule 41 **DO GOOD DESIGN**

What is good design? It's a question that has kept designers debating for decades. Usually it circles around questions of taste, fashion, or functionality. Whenever the conversation comes up, the "eye of the beholder" argument shuts it down. One person will say good design is design that "works," and another person will say what works depends on the individual user. At this point everyone nods and the conversation ends. But the question is never fully put to rest.

There's a deeper and more satisfying answer. Good design does not depend as much on the eye of the beholder as it does on a combination of aesthetics and ethics: Good design exhibits virtues. What virtues? Timeless human virtues such as generosity, courage, diligence, honesty, substance, clarity, curiosity, thriftiness, and wit. By contrast,

bad design is design that exhibits vices such as selfishness, fear, laziness, deceit, pettiness, confusion, apathy, wastefulness, and stupidity. In other words, we want the same things from design that we want from each other. When you combine ethics with aesthetics, you get good design.

Can you have a generous brand? A courageous company? A diligent algorithm? An honest product? Of course you can. Just as you can have a selfish business, a fearful policy, a lazy service, or a deceitful ad campaign. Good design is always aimed at long-term, broad success, whereas bad design settles for short-term, narrowly defined success. If design is change, then good design is change that benefits the largest number of people over the longest period of time.

Take responsibility for your work. Create positive outcomes that reach beyond the near and now. Practice good design. Be a genius.

Rule 42 BUILD SUPPORT METHODICALLY

It's one thing to be brilliant. It's another to convince people around you that your brilliance is viable. Of course, you can't blame them for shying away from risk. They may understand that every big idea starts out crazy, but they also know that every crazy idea doesn't end up big. They've seen what can happen when enthusiasm triumphs over caution.

Picture this scene: You bring an ingenious plan to your boss and say, "Sit down, boss. I've got a great new idea." You explain your plan in breathless detail. Your boss says, "Well, that certainly is a new idea. Who else has done this?"

"No one," you say. "That's the beauty of it!"

"Hardly," he says. "That's the *danger* of it. If we enact this plan, we could lose everything. Our business could disappear, we'll both be out of a job, and our company will be the laughingstock of the industry."

What went wrong here? Simple. You made the naïve assumption that your epiphany will be an epiphany to anyone else who hears about it. What you neglected to consider was that it took you weeks of thought, research, design, and redesign to arrive at your conclusion. In addition, you have years of experience and knowledge in your special discipline. Expecting your boss to "get it" without the same knowledge is unrealistic.

Imagine being shown a map of the world, only upside down, and being told that this is how all maps will be displayed in the future. Even though you know it's the same map you've seen a thousand times, it suddenly seems unfamiliar. It feels wrong.

I ALWAYS SAID SO

THIS IS AN INTERESTING BUT PERVERSE POINT OF VIEW

THIS IS TRUE BUT QUITE UNIMPORTANT

THIS IS WORTHLESS NONSENSE

It takes a bit of effort to accept the idea that Australia is "up over" instead of "down under."

Now imagine being presented with an idea that's guaranteed to turn your *actual* world upside down. It could be a radical new business initiative, a sweeping organizational change, or an offer of relocation to another country. Your first reaction might be resistance. You might cast around for logical arguments against it. Your whole body might be urging fight or flight.

A prerequisite for selling a new idea is to understand what geneticist J.B.S. Haldane knew when he charted the four stages of acceptance. Whenever a game-changing idea is presented, the first impulse of colleagues is to reject it as "worthless nonsense." As it starts to get traction, the same colleagues label it "interesting, but perverse." Later, when the idea is all but proven, they admit that "it's true, but unimportant." Finally, when success is assured, they claim "I always said so."

The trick is to condense the four stages into a shorter time span. If you can take your audience on the journey from "worthless nonsense" to "I always said so" in a matter of days instead of months, you may be able to keep the integrity of your idea as you gather broad support. The best way to condense the journey is with a story. The story can take the form of a fable, a comic strip, a children's book, or any other narrative vehicle. It can be illustrated with photos, drawings, charts, or videos. The main thing is to keep it simple. A deluge of facts will not win hearts and minds.

When you lead people from *what is* to *what could be* with a simple story, they can more easily imagine themselves playing a role. And if you give them a clear illustration of the happily-ever-after moment, they'll carry it in their minds as they go forward. Where there's a way, there's often a will.

Rule 43 **DON'T BLAME OTHERS**

Since the road to innovation is paved with mistakes, it's sometimes tempting to place the blame on others. Don't do it. Avoid pointing the finger, even when the problem is clearly not your fault. Take as much responsibility as you can.

By the same token, when you're working in a group, don't offload responsibility to others by "leaving the ball in their court." Try to keep the ball in your own court where you have control over it. And when you do send it over the net, follow it up to make sure it comes back.

There's something empowering about taking responsibility. You can make sure things are done

right while averting delays and misunderstandings.

Let's look at two examples. In our first example, Jason works in a group tasked with reimagining the customer experience for his company. He asks his subordinate Mark to conduct some observational research that they could both present at the next group session. Three days before the meeting, he learns that Mark's research won't be ready. John, now facing a disappointed group, explains that Mark has been late with his materials. The leader of the group reluctantly replaces both John and Mark with another team.

In our second example, at a broadcast company, Jennifer is working furiously to finalize a story for the evening news. Her computer crashes, erasing all her work. Earlier that day she had begged IT for help, but the technician never appeared. She calls her boss and sincerely apologizes for her embarrassing failure. Then she quickly locates an archived story to fill the scheduling hole, and sets about re-creating her story for a later program. A year later when her boss moves up to VP, Jennifer steps into her boss's role.

A benefit of taking responsibility is that you place yourself in a position of strength. People will tend to see you as a leader. They'll give you the benefit of the doubt, and the freedom to set things right.

You can be a genius all by yourself, but a genius without a community is not as powerful as a genius within a latticework of kindred spirits. As with any kind of lattice, whether physical, chemical, or social, it's the connections between the parts that determine the collective power of the whole—and therefore its value to the parts. In a social network, *how* you connect is everything.

There are two main ways to connect in a social network: *bonding* and *bridging*. Bonding is making friends with *like-minded* people—people of the same profession, the same political party, the same religion, the same nationality, or the same age. Bridging is making friends with *like-spirited* people —people from different backgrounds, but with similar ethics and ambition. Both kinds of connections are necessary to be successful and happy. But bridging is the activity that brings the highest rewards for innovators.

If you're seeking new information or insights, you'll need to look beyond your clique, since a clique is a closed system that acts more like a mirror than a window. Open the window. Connect with groups outside your circle. Put yourself in the way of meeting like-spirited people and not only like-minded people.

There's a popular saying that came from a Frank Sinatra song. It goes like this: If you can make it in New York, you can make it anywhere. While this may be true in some cases, for people in creative roles and niche businesses the opposite is more likely to be true: If you can't make it anywhere else, you can probably make it in New York. Large populations provide the social and business networks that can nurture professional success, especially when the profession is highly specialized or the specialist has rarified skills. You can perform in musicals in the state of Nebraska, but you'll learn much faster on the stages of New York.

Furthermore, studies show that people are happier in social networks. People near the center of a community tend to grow happier over time than those at the edges. This is because people in networks tend to share more knowledge. When you continually give away what you know, you learn to replenish your knowledge as you go, and you also benefit from the knowledge of others. Those who hoard knowledge don't get much knowledge back.

Genius is not so much something you *have* as something you *do*. You can believe you have genius in private, but you can't prove it unless you exercise it in public. The facts are clear: Excellence thrives in a network.

The arc of human evolution is really the arc of human learning. Our biology keeps improving, but only at a snail's pace. Our culture evolves much, much faster. The average IQ has edged upward in the last 50 years, whereas our biological brains have hardly changed at all in the last 50,000 years.

Most of us assume that learning difficult subjects requires a higher IQ, but it's more likely that a higher IQ comes from confronting difficult subjects. In a way, we don't solve problems—problems solve us. They help us complete the puzzle of who we are, asking us to stretch beyond our boundaries and confront what we don't know.

Genius, not evolution, is now the primary driver of progress. A genius is a person who takes creativity to the point of originality while creating better and more beautiful things—tools, objects, experiences, relationships, situations, solutions, and ideas. If the outcome is not beautiful, the maker is not demonstrating genius but mere creativity. Genius works on a higher level. It strives for elegance, ethics, and a level of quality that comes from mastery.

There's no set route to mastery. You can't print out a map or follow the instructions of your GPS device. The only voice that really matters is the

voice in your head, the one telling you to leap on this opportunity, avoid that trap, wait and see on that situation. In the pursuit of mastery, as in the geometry of nature, there are no straight lines—only curving, broken, sketchy, or tentative ones. The kind of learning that feeds your particular genius requires you take the scenic route, not the shortcut.

That doesn't mean you're without resources. A hiker may not know what kind of weather lies ahead, or what kind of terrain to expect, but she can start out with a general plan, be prepared with a backup plan, pack the right equipment, and arm herself with survival skills. Every step or misstep is provisional and correctable, a mini-lesson on the path to genius.

When you teach yourself, your learning is not part of a curriculum. There's no certificate, no graduation day. Just the satisfaction of following your joy until you become the person you're capable of being—the kind of person who aspires not just to *be* yourself but to *make more* of yourself—through learning, creativity, expression, influence, and love. You become the story you tell about yourself. Your story is your map.

We're not human beings; we're human becomings. We're not the sum of our atoms; we're the potential of our spirit, our vision, and our talent. We delight in feeling alive, in seeing what's possible, in putting our mark on the universe.

WE'RE NOT HUMAN BEINGS. WE'RE HUMAN BECOMINGS.

The first rule of genius is to break the rules. The last rule is to replace them with your own rules—variations drawn from your own experience, aligned with your own style of working. Rules are not laws. They're guidelines, and, as such, they must be seen as provisional.

All true invention, like all true art, is an act of protest, a rebellion against rules that have hardened into laws. Your job is to melt down the laws and recast them as principles that make sense to you, your discipline, and the needs of your work.

The 46 rules in this book are not the complete catalog. There are scores of others to be considered, tested, cherished, discarded, or recast. But these are ones that I've found to be most important in my own work, and to me they seem fairly universal. My immodest hope is that they'll serve as your inspiration as you create your own rules, your own set of tools, forged in the fires of your passion, perfectly balanced and fitted to your own hand.

ABOUT THE AUTHOR

Marty Neumeier is an advocate for creativity—whether in the service of brands, products, services, companies, environments, or communications. His stated professional goal is to bridge the distance between business and design. "Business is a fulcrum for change," he says. "Improving how business works is the quickest way to improve how the world works."

His 2003 book, *The Brand Gap*, redefined a brand as "a customer's gut feeling about a product, service, or organization," rejecting the widely held view that a brand was a logo or campaign promise. His follow-up book, *Zag*, introduced "onliness" as the true test of a brand strategy, and was named one of the "100 Best Business Books of All Time." His third book, *The Designful Company*, offered leaders a blueprint for building a culture of innovation.

Marty now serves as Director of Transformation for Liquid Agency, an international brand firm whose client list is a Who's Who of innovators. His vision for business creativity has led to engagements with some of the world's most innovative companies, including Apple, Google, Microsoft, Skype, Twitter, and Patagonia. From these experiences he has drawn the principles he shares in his publications, articles, lectures, and workshops.

In 2013, Marty published *Metaskills: Five Talents for the Robotic Age. Metaskills*, in a departure from his quick-read "whiteboard" books, goes deeply into the future of workplace creativity. It shows why—and how—we need to reeducate ourselves in the face of accelerating innovation. He wrote *The 46 Rules of Genius* as a "quick start guide" to *Metaskills*.

When Marty isn't working on a book or traveling for business, he spends his time in southwest France, where he and his wife keep a *petite maison*. To his embarrassment, he still has to bring a dictionary to the *supermarché*.